The Life of a Soldier During the Revolutionary War US History Lessons for Kids

Children's American History

Speedy Publishing LLC
40 E. Main St. #1156
Newark, DE 19711
www.speedypublishing.com

Once the British colonies in America decided to rebel against Great Britain's rule, the American Revolution occurred.

Read on and find out the interesting lives of the soldiers during the Revolutionary War!

The British were highly favored to win this war. Many battles were fought and these colonies were now free and this became an independent country we know as the United States. This war occurred from 1775 to 1783. Many soldiers' lives and their families were affected by this war.

The war began on April 19, 1775 in Massachusetts at Lexington and Concord. It lasted six years and ended when General Cornwallis surrendered at Yorktown, Virginia on October 19, 1781.

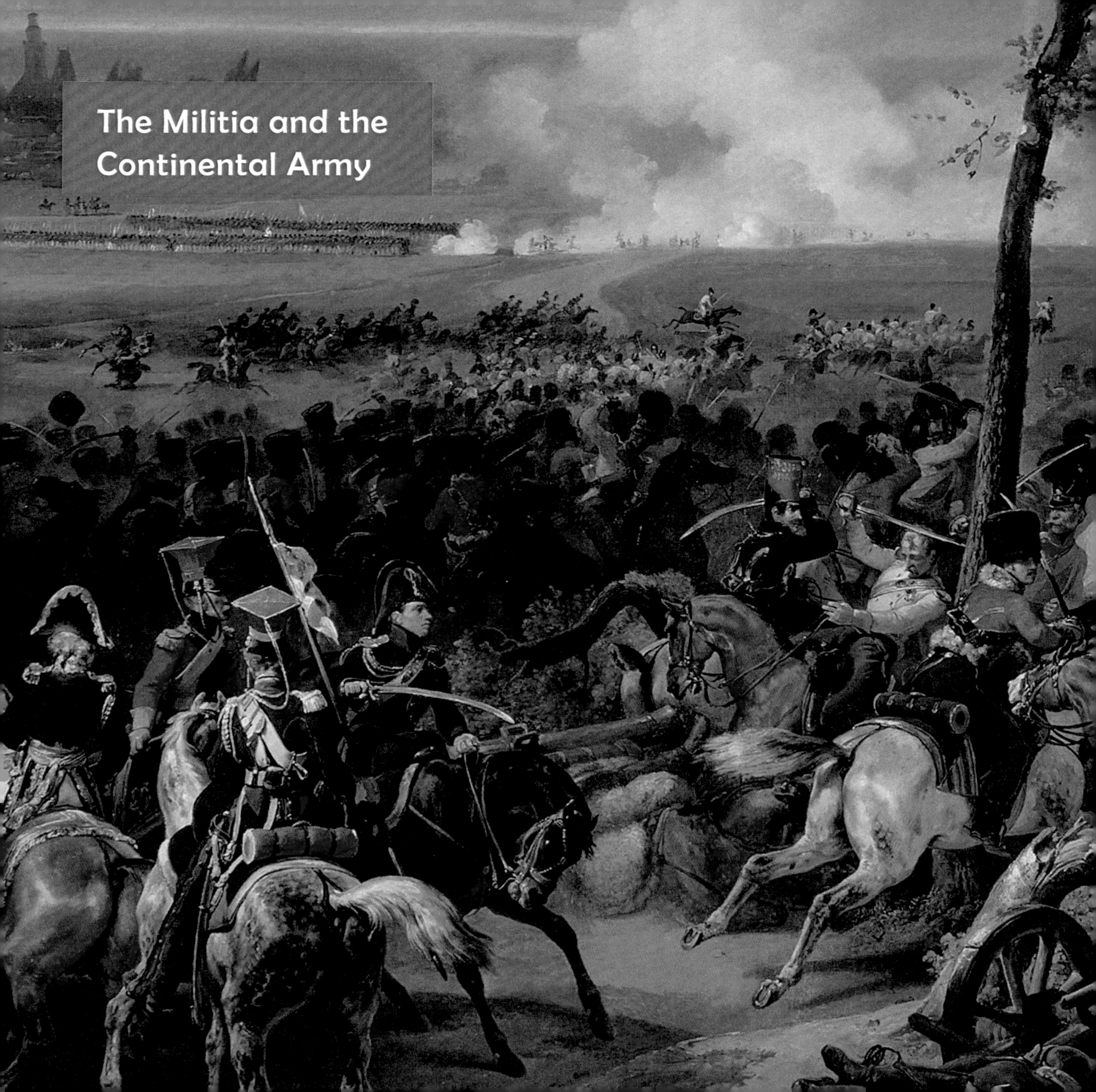

The Militia and the Continental Army

During this war, there were two groups of soldiers fighting this war, the militia and the Continental Army.

Citizens that were prepared to fight were known as the militia. To fight off Indian war bandits and parties, most communities and cities had a militia. It consisted of men between the age of 16 and 65, and they trained only a small number of times each year.

The Continental Army was established by the Continental Congress and was known as the first army of the U.S. George Washington became their commander. It consisted of volunteers that were paid, and they would enlist for a certain amount of time.

In the beginning, the enlistments were for a shorter time period of maybe six months. Later, the enlistments would last for up to three years. These soldiers trained as fighting soldiers.

How many were there?

The Continental Army consisted of up to 150,000 men that fought during the Revolutionary War. They did not serve all at the same time with the largest army consisted of approximately 17,000 men.

Were they paid?
When they enlisted, they were promised bounty at the end of their enlistment. This would be either money or land.

They would receive monthly pay as follows: privates $6, sergeants $8, and captains would receive $20. They also had to purchase their uniforms, weapons, and gear with their personal money.

Who joined the Continental Army?

The Continental Army consisted of farmers, preachers, tradesmen, and even some slaves. The slaves were offered freedom in exchange for fighting. Poor people found the land bounty a way to better their lives.

How old were they?

Their ages ranged from 18 to 24, even though there were younger boys and older men. The younger boys worked as water carriers, drummers, and messengers.

Medicine and Disease

During this war, disease caused more deaths than combat. They had a poor diet, clothes that were worn out, lived in wet shelters, and unsanitary conditions. Thousands of them died from smallpox and typhus.

During this era, hospitals and medicine did not have much to offer to protect them when they were suffering deadly sicknesses and combat injuries.

They were better off to not go to a doctor and let their injury heal on its own. Doctors even believed that cutting a person and letting their bad blood drain out would heal them!

What if a soldier was taken prisoner?
Because they were treated so badly, being taken as a prisoner was possibly one of the worst things to happen to them. The British treated them badly.

More than 8,500 soldiers died in prison, practically half of the deaths of Americans that took place during this war. They barely fed them and they were kept in disgusting, crowded conditions. May of the prisoners were in ships close to New York City.

Did women and children see battles? This war was fought wherever the two armies might meet up. This could be near towns or people's farmland.

Most people would flee their farms when the armies would arrive. At age 16, boys could enlist in the army. At the age of 7, boys could join as messengers or drummers. Molly Pitchers, consisting of women, took part in fighting.

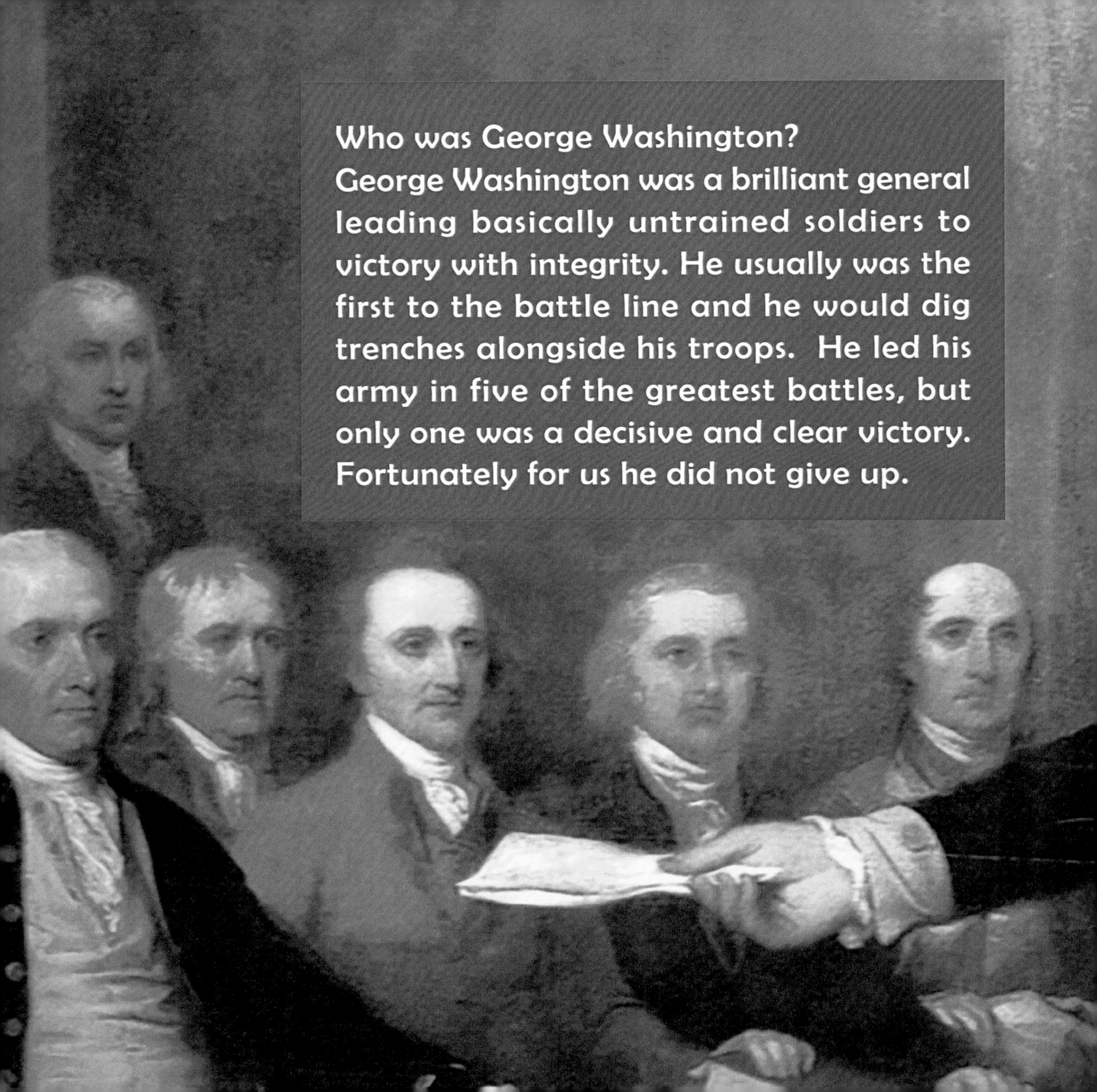

Who was George Washington?

George Washington was a brilliant general leading basically untrained soldiers to victory with integrity. He usually was the first to the battle line and he would dig trenches alongside his troops. He led his army in five of the greatest battles, but only one was a decisive and clear victory. Fortunately for us he did not give up.

George Washington then served as our first president and served from 1789 to 1797.

He stepped down after two terms consisting of eight years. He felt that he should not become powerful for too long. Since then only Franklin D. Roosevelt has served longer than two terms.

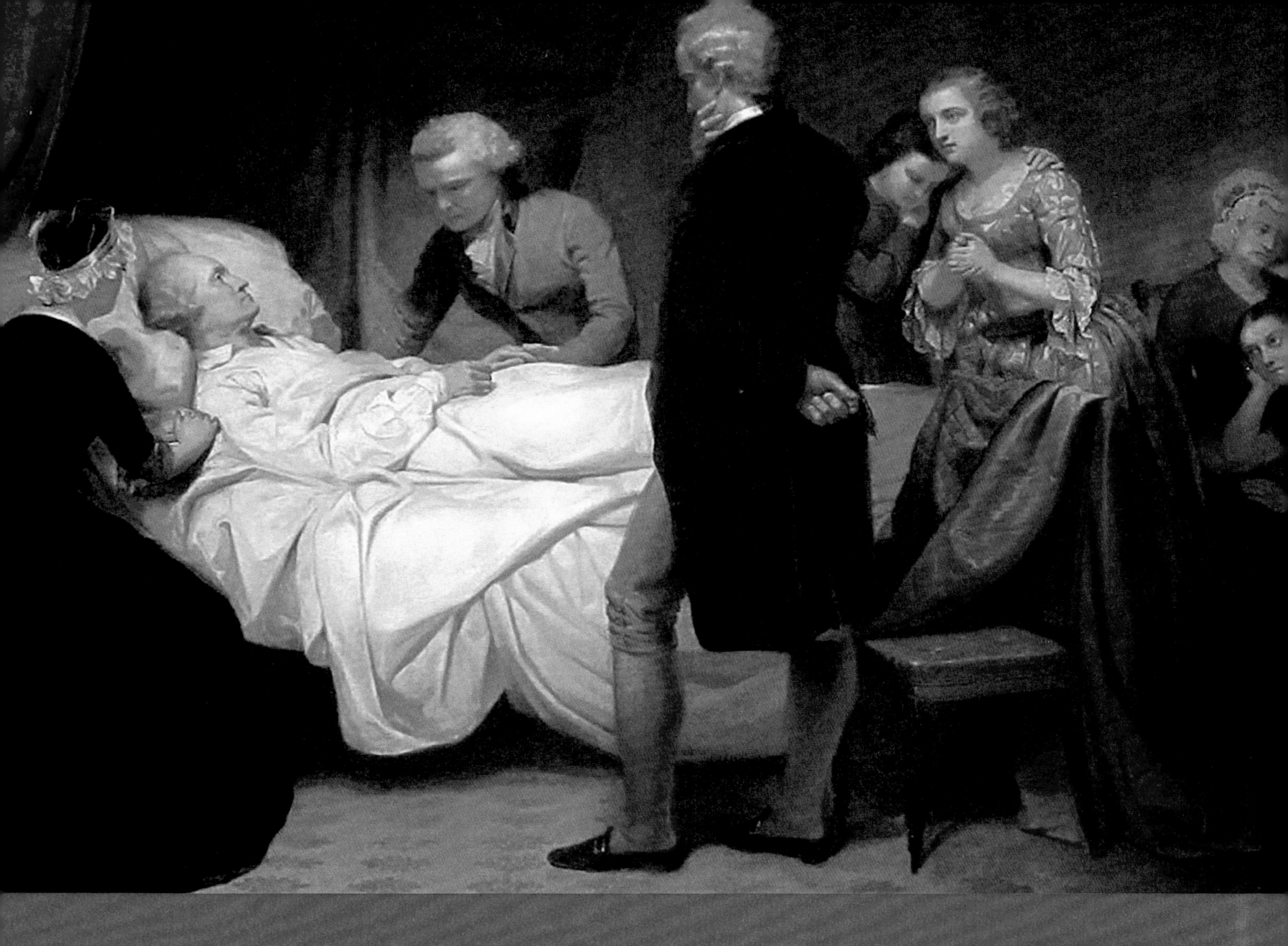

He died shortly after leaving office on December 14, 1799. He caught a nasty cold which turned into an infection in his throat, causing his death.

Did You Know?
Hessians were British soldiers that came here from Hesse, located in Germany.

Many of these soldiers felt that if it was not for the leadership of General Washington, they would have left the army because of the bad conditions.

A lot of the mothers, children, and wives of the soldiers followed them. They would sew their clothes, cook their meals, tended to them if they were sick, and would wash their clothes. Communication was often delayed by days and even weeks because it was delivered in person.

British General Burgoyne hatched a plan during the summer of 1777 to combine their troops and two others in New York. If this plan worked, it probably would have ended the war. They were blocked by over 10,000 American Patriots.

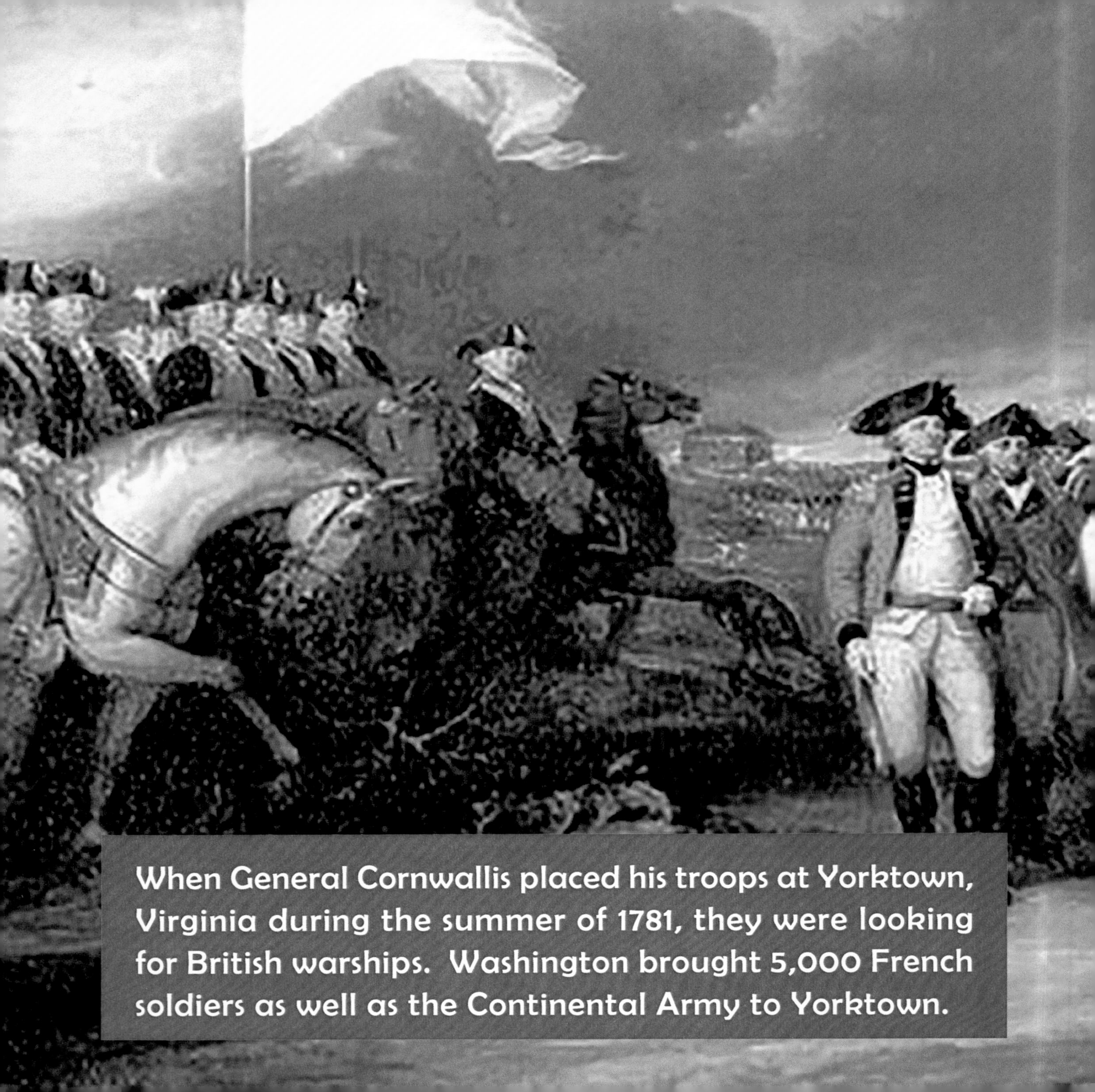

When General Cornwallis placed his troops at Yorktown, Virginia during the summer of 1781, they were looking for British warships. Washington brought 5,000 French soldiers as well as the Continental Army to Yorktown.

At this time, the French fleets naval fleets drove off of the British ships. They were trapped. Cornwallis then surrendered on October 19, 1871 and the Americans had then won the war.

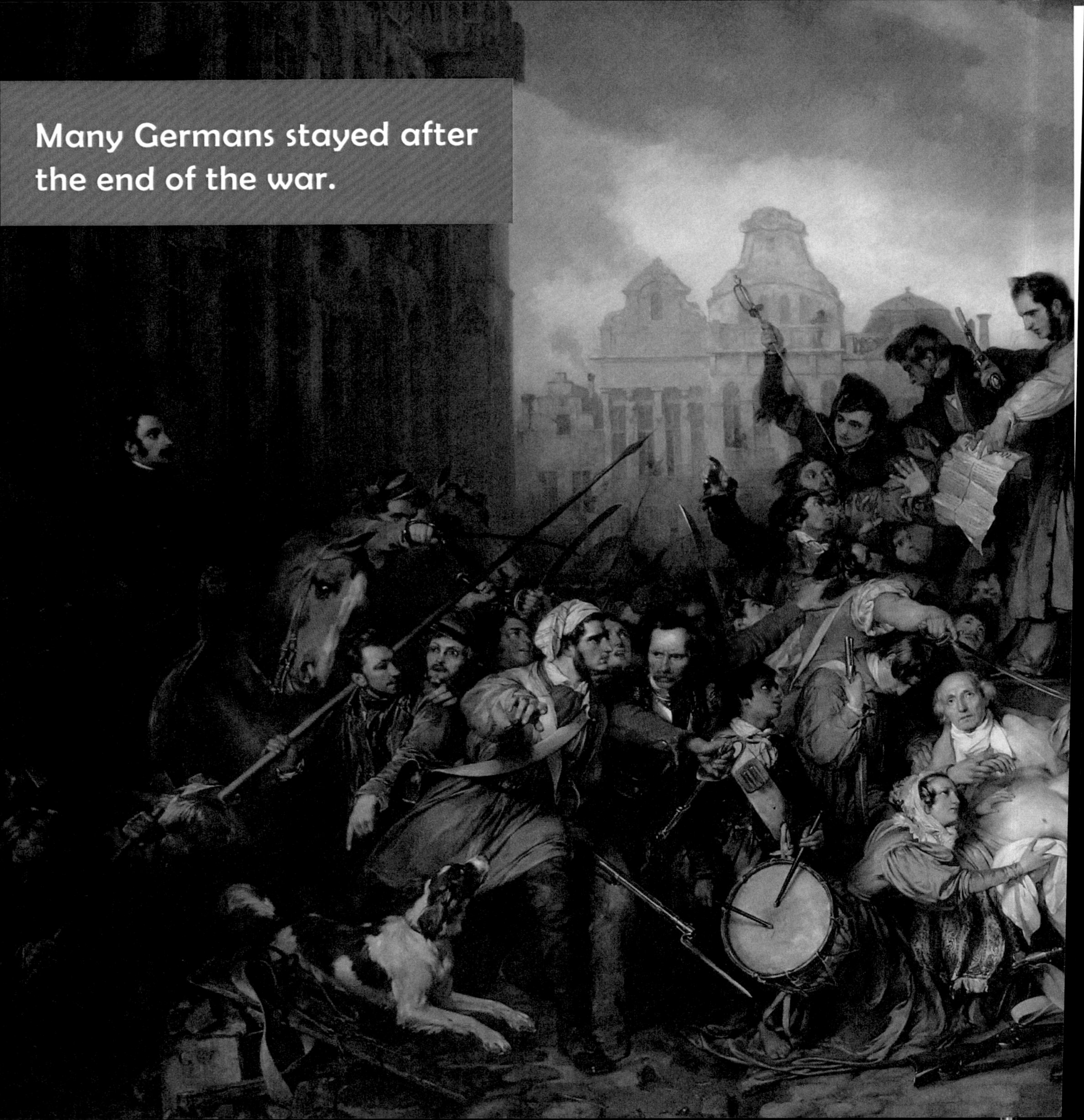

Many Germans stayed after the end of the war.

Why do they wear uniforms?
In battle, uniforms are important so the soldiers know who is on their side, that way they do not shoot someone that is fighting on the same side.

The musket was the main weapon during this war. These weapons give off a white smoke cloud when fired and the battlefield would be coated with the white smoke. Because of this, many of the armies liked wearing bright colors so they would be able to tell their friends from their enemies.

Uniforms also provide information as to the ranking of the soldiers by their stripes, badges, and piping on their coats and the hats. This also provides information as to who is in charge.

American Uniforms

The local militia became the American soldiers and not only were they not trained, they also did not have uniforms.

Congress adopted brown as the official uniform color in 1775, but due to a lack of material, most of them did not have the brown coats. If they were in the same regiment they would wear the same color. Blue and gray were also popular colors.

Their uniform would include a wool coat with cuffs and a collar, a hat turned up on one side, a shirt made of linen or cotton, vest, leather shoes, and breeches.

British Uniforms

Since their uniforms consisted of coats that were bright red, the British were called the "Red Coats." During the Revolutionary War they would occasionally wear blue uniforms.

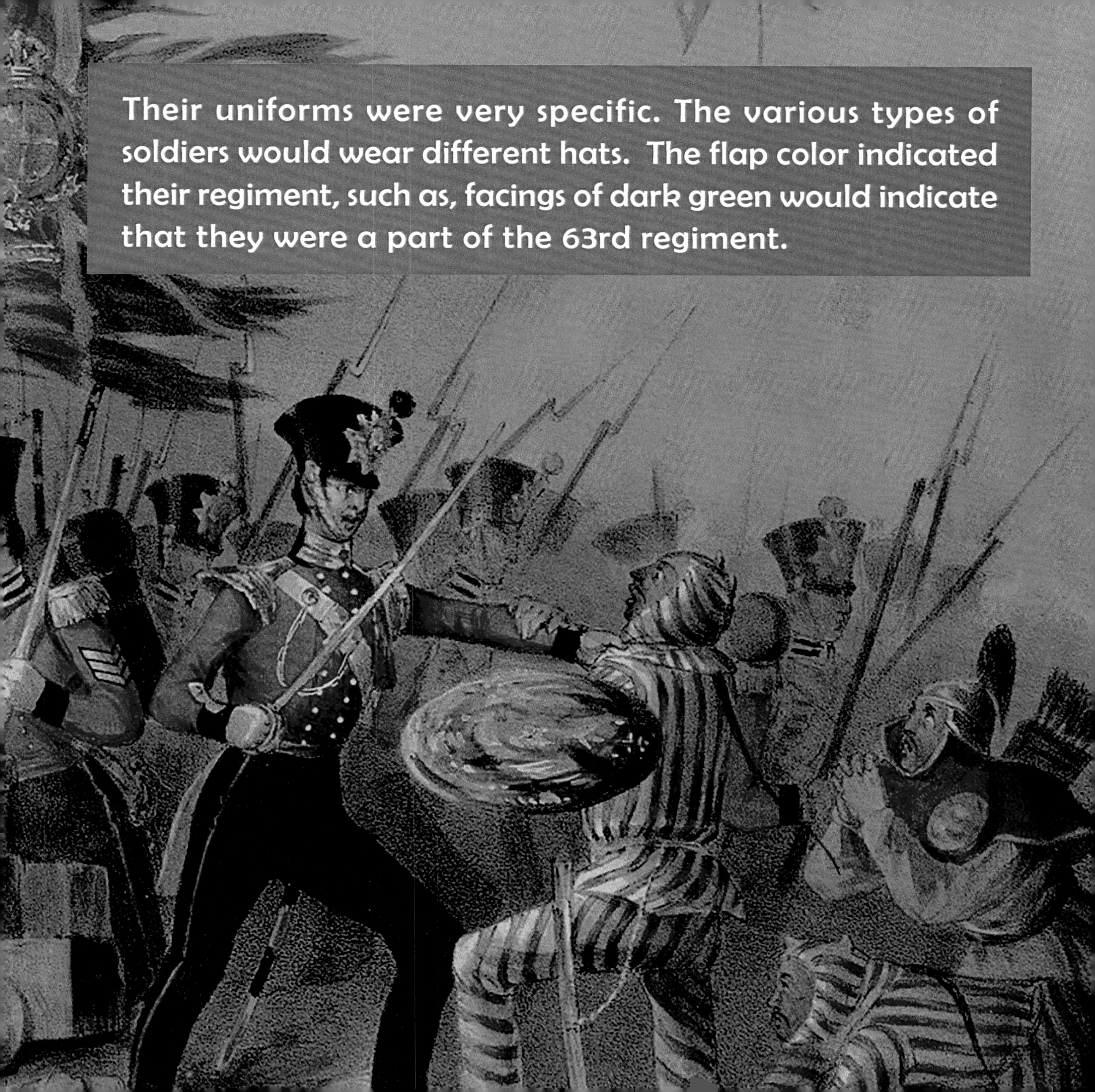

Their uniforms were very specific. The various types of soldiers would wear different hats. The flap color indicated their regiment, such as, facings of dark green would indicate that they were a part of the 63rd regiment.

The musket became their most vital weapon. They could load the musket and fire it three times in a minute. The muskets fired lead balls and was considered a bore weapon.

Since these weapons were not very accurate, regiments would fire them simultaneously in order to cover a big area.

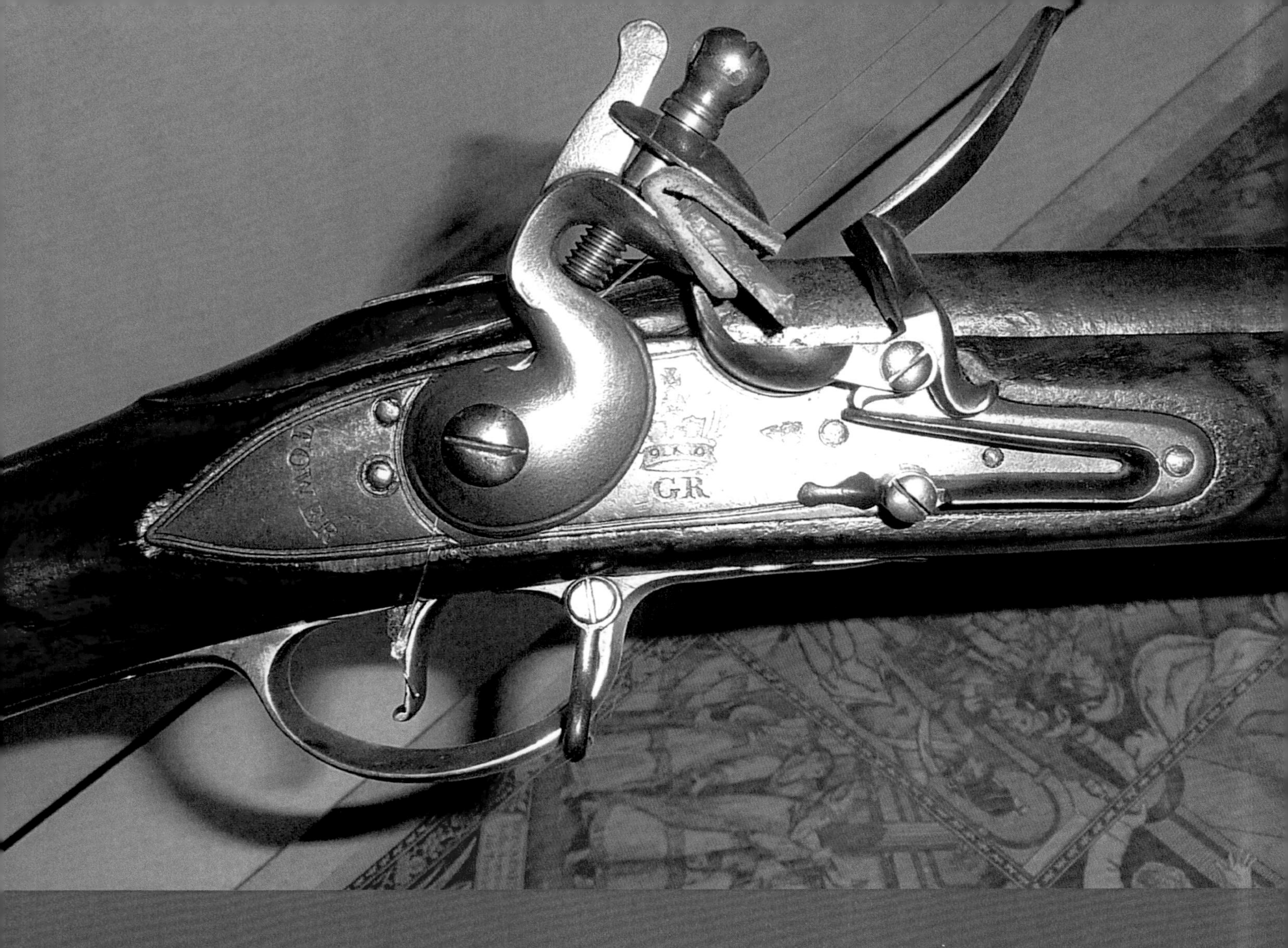

The "Brown Bess" was the most well-known musket owned by British soldiers, and most of the American soldiers owned ones that had been captured or stolen from the British.

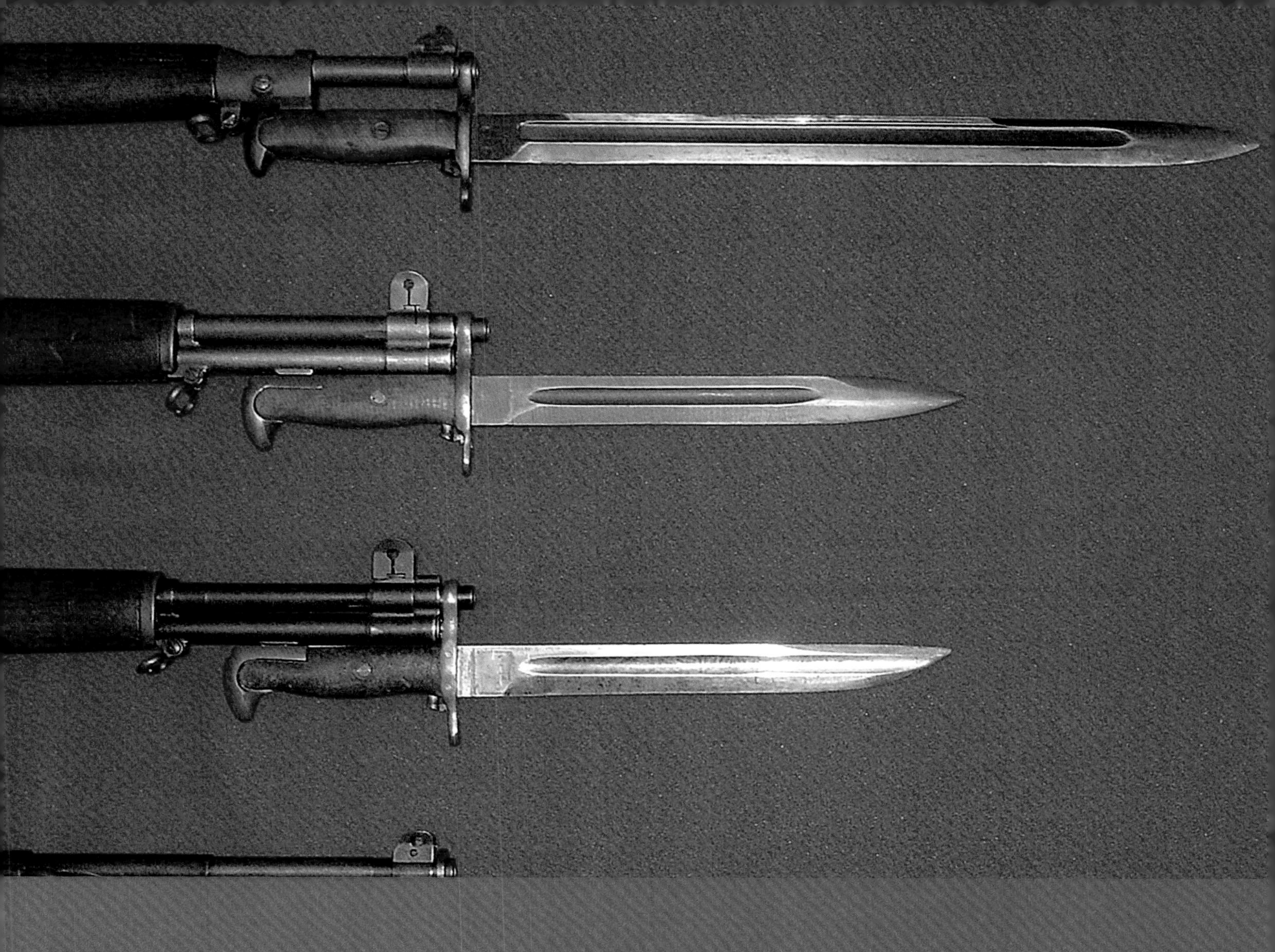

When the enemy would come within a close distance, they would fight using a sharp blade connected to the end of a musket and this was called a bayonet.

Soldiers would also bring knapsacks or haversacks (similar to a backpack) which would hold their clothing, blanket, and food, ammo and a canteen.

Interesting Facts About Their Uniforms and Gear

"Lobster backs" became another name for the British since their coats were red.

The French uniforms were white and had different colors of blue for their coats and jackets.

Shoes became most difficult to maintain and they would often wear them out on marches and would continue the march barefoot.

In the 1700s, dyes would fade quickly and while we see images of them in their red coats, more than likely the colors would have faded.

You can find much more information about the Revolutionary War on the internet and by going to the library as well as asking questions of your teachers, parents, and friends.

Visit
BABY PROFESSOR
EDUCATION KIDS
www.BabyProfessorBooks.com
to download Free Baby Professor eBooks
and view our catalog of new and exciting
Children's Books